THE ADDICTION

A Children's Guide to Understanding the Dynamics of Drugs and Alcohol

Written by Janet Amptman, MA, MFT, LADC
Illustrator David Amptman
Co Illustrator Janet Amptman
© 2013

This book is for children ages five years and older to help them understand the dynamics of chemical dependency. Children may be socially exposed to chemically dependent people in many different ways. The sooner they understand chemical dependency by approaching this issue head on the sooner it gives them the tools to not be at risk themselves and to not internalize the problems they may see socially or privately. Just saying no doesn't explain the lure of drugs and alcohol and the complex problems associated with them.

This book is for any parent who is seeking guidance on how to talk to their child about the sensitive issue of a spouse or relative addicted to drugs and/or alcohol or just to generally educate their children about this topic. Reading this book to a child is taking a proactive stance to help inoculate their child against the addiction cycle of shame and blame and to reduce the risk that they themselves will become chemically dependent.

It may also be helpful to explore the various aspects of chemical dependency discussed in the book with a recovery counselor or psychotherapist, and /or child therapist. This book is also to help children understand that chemical dependency is not their fault. It is also not about whether or not their parent loves them. Addiction is not about lack of love but obsession, compulsion and loss of control. It is an illness, a brain disorder.

Narrative therapy, developed by Michael White and David Epston, is a form of therapy where a person learns to change the problem saturated story they have created about themselves to one that affirms life choices. One intervention used in Narrative therapy is a process called externalizing the problem which is having the problem (in this case chemical dependency) defined as a separate entity from the person. In simple terms, according to Narrative therapy "the person is not the problem the problem is the problem". This book is a form of externalizing the problem, a powerful therapeutic tool intended to reduce shame and blame.

Acknowledgements

I never could have written this book without the constant encouragement and love of my amazing and artistic husband of twenty four years, David and my wonderful children Elijah and Kya. Both my children gave constructive criticism to help me see more through a child's eyes and helped to make this book what it is. My parents, Richard and Frieda, who have always been there and my mom who is an artistic inspiration. My supportive family and friends. My consultants Dr. Robert Epstein, Dr. Stephanie Dillon and Sherry Wright, LMFT who have helped me through many difficult moments and helped to give me the confidence to be where I am at today. My supportive colleagues throughout the years Elizabeth Dear, MFT, Dr. Laurie Drucker, Pamela Feldstein-Mayne, Lauren Greenwood, LMFT, Frank Lemus, LMFT, Sandra Poupeney, LCSW, and Renee Reveles, LCSW. The late Dr. Kaye Rossi, who was a dear friend and colleague who devoted her life's work to addiction and wrote her thesis on the subject. My colleague Dr. Chuck Holt, who got me writing again. The many friends and clients who have lost their lives to chemical dependency and the children clients I have worked with that have struggled with their parents not being there because of drugs and alcohol.

Painting by: Frieda Klein

Butterfly...
one day
at a time

-Christopher Patchel, Modern Haiku, 39:1

I love my
mommy so much!

But sometimes she acts funny and can be really mean. I often want to play with her in the morning but she just can't seem to wake up and when she finally does she is grumpy.

She is grumpy until she goes into the bathroom for a while and then gets her special drink which makes her breath smell funny. Then she is happy for a while. She starts spilling her drink and walking funny then she often yells about things and I don't understand why. Sometimes I feel she hates me or doesn't love me.

Mommy always fights with her boyfriends.

She and her friends and boyfriends spend a lot of time in her bedroom and when I want her attention she tells me to leave them alone. I see so many people come in and out of our house, who are they?

My mom doesn't come home for days and the neighbors or my grandparents have to take care of me.

My mommy hasn't come home for weeks. I went to visit her at a park and she looked different. She was really thin and had red spots on her face.

I was brought to a man, a therapist, who told me he would help me talk about my mom in a safe place.

When we got to talking, it just popped out "I hate my mom, she doesn't love me. She loves her special drink more. Why won't she take care of me? She doesn't love me. Maybe if I was better and didn't make her mad she wouldn't have left."

That therapist guy said "your mommy does love you but she has been tricked by the addiction monster".

He explained what alcohol and drugs are and how it, the addiction monster, changes people from what is truly in their hearts.

Your mom is having a fight inside her, one that is saying to the addiction monster, leave me alone and the other that is tricked by the monster believing she cannot live without him and wants to hug him.

He told me every time she lets the addiction monster in through drinking her special drink or doing drugs she gets brain washed or tricked and forgets you, her job, her family and it makes her mean. It's like when you want cookies or candy and an adult says "no" but you take it anyway, sneak it or throw a temper tantrum. You do this even though you know it's bad for your teeth, that you act differently by jumping around or getting mad when you can't have it. It's like the candy or cookies have control of you just like drugs and alcohol with your mom but for her much worse.

The addiction monster is bigger than your mom. It tricks her and won't go away. Your mom wants it to go away too but she can't fight the monster alone.

To get rid of the addiction monster she has to get help like at a hospital, in a meeting of adults or with a counselor. You can't do anything to make her better or to beat the monster. Adults have to help her do that.

He said your job is to take good care of yourself by doing the things you love every day, do good in school, think of your calm safe place, and take deep breaths. Boy, oh boy, was that therapist guy smart.

My mom finally did get help. She went to a hospital and now I have my mommy back but she won't be able to take care of me until we are sure the addiction monster is gone. My mommy has to meet with adults every week to beat the addiction monster and to make sure he never comes back. She should never have her special drink or drugs again. It will call to her and she has to continue to fight it.

That therapist guy told me some
kids parents never get help
and don't quit using drugs and
alcohol, some go to jail and
some get help but get tricked
by the addiction monster again
and some beat him.

"Bad things don't have to happen to people who have a problem with drugs and alcohol; there is always hope for being rescued from the addiction monster. If you find yourself afraid or worried about your mommy or daddy, find a grown-up you trust to talk to about your fears."

I meet with that therapist guy weekly to help remind me to take good care of myself no matter what and to have a safe place to talk about my feelings about my mom and the addiction monster.

Things to Help Me Feel Better

1. **Breathing** - Breathe in through the nose for five seconds while pushing out the belly, hold for five seconds and blow out the mouth for seven seconds while sucking the belly in. Repeat exercise 10 times.

2. **Self-Soothing** - With eyes closed and taking deep breaths think of a calm safe place. Picture the sights, sounds, smells and feeling of the calm safe place.

3. **Mindfulness Meditation** - With eyes open let your mind go blank. Notice every time you hear a sound, see a sight or feel something on your body (like a breeze). Say to yourself when you notice each sensation "sight, sound or touch" and take notice as to what happens. Do this for a few minutes.

4.   **Self-Soothing** - Hold your teddy bear or dolly tight to calm you.

5.   **Positive Self Talk** - Your mind is like play dough you get to decide if it is going to be a positive or negative shape by the things you say to yourself. Some positive examples "I choose to feel good", "stop the stinking thinking", "use my words" and "I love myself, I'm awesome".

6.   **Self-Soothing** - Tap your left leg with your left arm then your right leg with your right arm back and forth to music until the song ends.

Recommended Resources for Parents

Al-Anon & Al-Ateen crisis line
1-800-344-2666

Alcohol Helpline
1-877-589-4611

Betty Ford Center
(ask for Children's Program)
1-800-854-9211
www.bettyfordcenter.org

Website provides resources for children of alcoholics and addicts.
Children's program offers intensive prevention and education groups
for children whose lives have been impacted by a loved ones'
addiction to alcohol or other drugs.

National Crisis Hotline
1-877-235-4525

National Marijuana Hotline
1-800-766-6779

Narcotics Anonymous
(drug addiction hotline)
1-800-317-3222

National Association for Children of Alcoholics
1-888-554-2627
www.nacoa.org – go to the tab: Just For Kids

A national nonprofit organization working to help
children of alcohol and drug dependent parents. Their website
has a special link for kids as well as important information for parents.

Made in the USA
Las Vegas, NV
26 August 2021

28935524R00031